MORE PRAISE FOR *FATHER ELEGIES*

"*Father Elegies* by Stella Fridman Hayes is unforgettable. Poems that disassemble and reassemble us with their history, trajectory, and resilience. Poems that move and stand still simultaneously like the breath of languages, stories, and selves the poet has sculpted. This is a fiercely passionate and aesthetically expansive collection by a daring poet."

—NATHALIE HANDAL, author of *Life in a Country Album*

"Impressively rangey and formally clever, Stella Hayes' *Father Elegies* invites us into perhaps the most intimate of losses. That invitation gives us access not just to the hospital room or the funeral, but even to 'The scar tissue in folds growing.' A powerful and emotionally vulnerable collection that grows deeper with each reading."

—KYLE McCORD, author of *In a Time of Impending Doom*

"How can we begin to grapple with the pain of the past? In *Father Elegies*, Stella Hayes excavates the landscape of childhood and grief with astonishing power. She moves across languages and forms like a true artist and uses her dexterity with both to capture intimate portraits of loved ones from the past: a mother who '[w]ash[es] grief out / Of hair,' a father who is 'breaking up a fistfight or a universe.' A stunning poetry collection that will leave you illuminated long after you put it down."

—WENDY CHEN, author of *Their Divine Fires*

"It is amazing and, sometimes, miraculous that the wounds of memory can be healed by memory. And yet such a miracle is the eternal task of language: to be both a temporal wound and an enduring cicatrix. In these *Father Elegies*, Stella Hayes outspeeds death upon the jagged surfaces of history and of syllables. Her task is beautifully accomplished."

—DONALD REVELL, author of *The English Boat*

"Like Hamlet speaking to the ghost of his father, Stella Hayes presents language as both obstacle and bridge, and these heartbreaking poems remind us that the 'simplicity of death / is always surprising.' Despite the tragedies that shape *Father Elegies,* a farewell song to a larger-than-life father, or perhaps because of them, Hayes's voice rings clear, her images astonish, her palpable language and inborn music pull us through from start to end. This book will change your life."

—JENNIFER MILITELLO, New Hampshire Poet Laureate

WHAT BOOKS PRESS

AN IMPRINT OF

THE GLASS TABLE

COLLECTIVE

LOS ANGELES

ALSO BY STELLA HAYES

One Strange Country

FATHER ELEGIES

FATHER ELEGIES

STELLA HAYES

WHAT
BOOKS
PRESS

LOS ANGELES

Library of Congress Cataloging-in-Publication Data

Names: Hayes, Stella, author.
Title: Father Elegies / Stella Hayes.
Description: Los Angeles : What Books Press, 2024. | Summary: "The author
    considers the role of legacy-from familial history to the inheritances
    of literature, art, and culture-in shaping the self, offering a fraught
    origin story that ultimately transcends the personal"-- Provided by
    publisher.
Identifiers: LCCN 2024022653 | ISBN 9798990014930 (paperback)
Subjects:
Classification: LCC PS3608.A9435 F38 2024 | DDC 811/.6--dc23/eng/20240520
LC record available at https://lccn.loc.gov/2024022653

Cover art: Gronk, *Untitled*, mixed media on paper, 2023
Book design by ash good, www.ashgood.com

What Books Press
363 South Topanga Canyon Boulevard
Topanga, CA 90290

WHATBOOKSPRESS.COM

For my father,
Grigory Mihaylovich Fridman (1931-1981)

CONTENTS

PAHA (NOUN, RUSSIAN)
WOUND

ОТЧАЯНИЕ (NOUN, RUSSIAN)
DESPAIR

What I hope (when I hope) is that we'll see each other again,—

—To the Dead, Frank Bidart

She is the one who owns the terror.

—*Absolom, Absolom*, William Faulkner

NESCHASTEYE (NOUN, RUSSIAN)

MISFORTUNE

IN LOSS'S MOTION

You were like a feudal lord, hair back, sword drawn on
A shiny red bicycle, cutting the air into slashes. It was hardly enough,

The air would stop. Breathing hardly enough for half
A person. If I could breathe my first & last breath in you, I would

You would siphon off electricity from the electric grid,
So that we could have what was left of enlightenment.

How our Russian vinyl records were heard from the turntable,
The one you would crank up in the afternoons, that drowned

Out the stew's song simmering on low heat in the kitchen.
Laughter's shaft of memory sounds out the nudity

Of winter. On drives to Kyiv, I would count receding power
Lines, connected to a nuclear power station in the newly-built

Town. Root vegetables grew with flourish in collective,
Commercial fields, outside our apartment. Now, not sparing

Any air for myself, I would swallow fire wrapped
In fire for you. I'm not far — somewhere, Father,

You're breaking up a fistfight or a universe, & I predict
You'll break my heart in an uneven number.

REGARDING HIS HEART

I eavesdrop on the sounds
Of his heart, which cardiologists describe
As a closed fist & the weight of a 2-liter bottle of Coke

A heart, sounded by a rhythmic thump,
Reverberates out of four hollowed cavities,
Carrying air. His, used to open

Like a map. I would put my ear
To the left ventricle, behind a collapsing
Hospital door. His was extraordinary,

Missing roadways for air to pass,
To make him rich with air again. It's divided
Into four chambers, a right & left, two atria

& two ventricles. The atria thirsty for more
& more. The ventricles resigned to pump
Without interruption. His superior & inferior

Venae cavae weren't cutting it. A mystery
Undisturbed. The parts that couldn't
Be saved or returned to us

HEART, СЕРДЦЕ (SERDZE), HIS SONG

Как много девушек хороших
>Alas, there are many lovely young women in the world

Как много ласковых имён
>Each with a tender name

Но лишь одно из них тревожит
>Yet only one among them is the source of my unrest

Унося покой и сон — когда влюблён
>Stirring me out of calm & sleep — when I'm in love —

Любовь нечаянно нагрянет
>By chance, love makes its visit

Когда её совсем не ждёшь
>— When I least expect it

И каждый вечер сразу станет удивительно хорош
>Instantly making each night a joy —

И ты поёшь
>And you sing!

Припев
>Chorus

Сердце — тебе не хочется покоя
>Be still my heart

Сердце — как хорошо на свете жить
>Heart — it is a joy to be alive

11

ROOT CELLAR

Down you took me my hand gripping yours
Underlying a girl's abundant fears

You were a gentle person, leading me down
Steps that smelled of a cement mixture innovated by the Romans

But of no use in this aging infrastructure of tract
Identical apartment buildings with damp root cellars

Storing jarred, pickled cucumbers
That would become half-sours & full-sours, tomatoes

With skin ruinous, as you take it to the mouth,
Carrots, beets & potatoes that would grow

Horns that we would cut off with a knife & eat
Too old. There were mushrooms

Foxlike, orange-brown, foraged in the local forest
That we would drive to in our Fiat made for the Soviet consumer

That brand new seemed second-hand. Crocodile-
Green, with fabric seats, a radio & a stick shift that was too hard

To drive. Too physically demanding for someone
With a wracked heart. The root cellar was divided

Into a multitude of parcels like the vineyards
In the Côte d'Or. Neighbors sticking to an implied code of honor

Of never stealing the enervated vegetables. Steering clear
Of what did not belong to the neighbor on each side

You were one of them later.
In the beginning, you were a thoroughbred, an amateur boxer

In the lightweight division. Fighting icicles, cutting up
Snow. Our family frozen in time —

The refrigerator plant you managed, sheltered a dream
Of leaving one day for good, with us

One day landing into a happy ending,
A refrigerator full —

Of America,
Lined with large-scale manufactured foods

Eggs, red-skinned onions, butter, milk
Lacking you Father, to show me my way

IN SHADOW OF NIGHT

A grieving child's   wounds are small to measure, not yet
rounded out by time. The scar   tissue in folds growing
alongside a tall femur. My   mother must not have seen me

beginning to grieve my stuffed animals.
As I fell to the night, each night, I made my own
archeological dig, out of the   wall. It gave in

to the nail in my forefinger willingly. I wounded the wall
nightly & no one noticed. My wall   in the living room that
doubled as a bedroom. The sofa bed that opened nightly.

My   mother &   father mapping
out, in secret, a way out

WISHBONE

He was the mother I never had. We slept in beds joined by proximity. One night he fed me fish, a bone got away from its hardened flesh, & struck me in the throat. I can remember still how he believed he had lost me to something so small, a sharp object between us. It was his one wrong move. She — on the night shift — on the other side of a wheat field. While we slept, she re-read the Russian canon, all night — away from weighty shadows, waking up into morning. The girl looking up at ruins. Shooting arrows at the heart shot *instinctively*. That's all I have left, a fishbone. A wish.

RAZLUKA

I didn't want to be separated from you when the school day ended
     cutting through a wheat field to get home.

I would double-skip the wide concrete stairs which lay in my way
     like tombstones. I would peel into the apartment,

Out of breath, thirsty. You would wait for me —,
     holding a glass full of water, sweaty with cold.

I conjure you reading *Pravda* in the kitchen sitting on a stool —,
     looking for *truth*.

You would curate me as your daughter, molding my heart
     to look & feel like yours. The music we listened

To was almost Western. Anna German, a Polish singer who sang
     accentless Russian elegiacally —.

Where are you, Father?
You have been dead for so long —

DARK NIGHT, (ТЁМНАЯ НОЧЬ), HER SONG

In the dark night, only bullets rage through the steppe
Тёмная ночь, только пули свистят по степи,
As night howls through electrical wires, dulling flickering stars
Только ветер гудит в проводах, тускло звёзды мерцают...

In the dark my beloved, you're not asleep
В тёмную ночь ты, любимая, знаю, не спишь,
As you wipe away tears beside a cradle in secret
И у детской кроватки тайком ты слезу утираешь.

I adore the depth of your loving eyes
Как я люблю глубину твоих ласковых глаз,
As I dream of pressing against them — if only once — with my lips
Как я хочу к ним прижаться хоть раз губами!

As the night, my beloved, divides us
Тёмная ночь разделяет, любимая, нас,
As the heart-broking dark steppe is stretched out before us
И тревожная, чёрная степь пролегла между нами.

I believe in you, my dearest companion
Верю в тебя, в дорогую подругу мою,
With this conviction, I am safe from a bullet
Эта вера от пули меня тёмной ночью хранила

Happily, I am at peace during a near fatal battle
Радостно мне, я спокоен в смертельном бою:
Knowing that you will meet me with a loving heart — no matter what
Знаю, встретишь с любовью меня, что б со мной ни случилось.

I don't fear death, we crossed paths not once in the steppe
Смерть не страшна, с ней встречались не раз мы в степи...
Even now, as it is upon me
Вот и теперь надо мною она кружится,

Sleepless, you wait for me at our daughter's bedside
Ты меня ждёшь и у детской кроватки не спишь,
And I know that nothing will harm me
И поэтому знаю, со мной ничего не случится!

TEMPERA

We drove through a field of white on white, a light held back from light. The birch forest made a clearing —. As a boy-in-mourning, Yuri Zhivago climbed up on his mother's grave on the morning of her burial. The dead soil giving in —, to dead soil. The grave, a lightless hump. With outstretched neck & head turned up to a heavenly body, he performed a movement that, to the crowd, gathered looked like the beginning of a *howl*. *I howled like a wolf cub as a girl at Papa's funeral.* The airless winter morning rehearsed its own ending. Lumping lumps of snow were cleared by the gravedigger for his grave. When I feel the wet heaviness of snow on my retreating hand, I think of Yuri's disappearance, the snow & Pasternak refusing his Nobel Prize. Won't you give up on me —. I keep secrets as they keep me.

ELEGY FOR WINTER

Her boiled-wool boots were packed with purpose. A first winter in Orenburg's inhuman cold. A one-sided stare into dread. The open snowed-in field she had to cross, rifle tucked close to her heart & lunch in pail. The same pail, one of two that in the summer she would fill with water from a nearby well & bring home, strung on rope over her shoulders —. The wolves howled in near distance. Their eyes reflected a worn red light. They wanted to huddle close to her beauty, her emptiness. Each day unfolding & contracting. The day like her heart, emptied of promise. Her eyes fixed on the future —

LUDA, THE GIRL WHO WAS MY BEST FRIEND

Dressed in school uniforms, finely ironed by each of our mothers. Detachable starched stiff white Victorian collars around our necks. We would skip on a fresco of hopscotch. New concrete, erasing a small-town dirt road. We'd pick bright-colored chalk from a box of cardboard, our fingers covered in radioactive ash. How streaks of it end up on our faces, giving our nightly baths a painterly glow. Every day after school I'd go up to see her. I remember her a year or so older. A blond girl. I had more *pupsiki*, small rubbery Germanmade dolls — intricate, free. In their underwear & wardrobe of tiny dresses, sweaters, hats, shoes. We undressed & dressed them. Small choices in a country dispossessed of the *I*. In her home, voices were hushed, plans were made in daylight. When my parents confided in 9-year-old me the dangerous news that we were leaving, I couldn't tell her. We played, combed & rearranged each other's hair into monarchal braids. I wanted to leave my plastic friends for her but if I did, she would tell her parents. Maybe it started then, in Brovary, Ukraine, I liked blue eyes more than brown. Diaspora, my love

IF ONLY / IF ONLY

I am leaving a line as you leave a single wall / up to a house
    Before   (it is)   demolished

No matter where I go / I imagine
    Nearly   what / I remember

Maybe I / imagin(ed) him / my lyric / my flesh / my obsession
    My holy subject / my sole / certain destroyer

                    Time   rotates   in revolutions
                    Clockwise   on my wrist

                    Papa's *Raketa*   wristwatch / alloyed
                    Thinly rests   on the nightstand

                    Colliding with   my (re)collection
                    I'm struck   as I strike

      Beats & coils of time / against faces
On coins of the state's   statesmen

      Is it spring / yes   let's say it is
The lilac still life / dying   on the nightstand

      If only / If only / I imagine
I make my way back in ,,

      I climb   inside the oak wardrobe
      Like the fastest fox in a forest
      Looking for coins   loose change

      My hand falling in one   pocket & another
      Of his electrical engineer suit   made
      Of Soviet   military-weight wool

Each night   refilling   pockets   with coins
For me / It must have been for me
My hand   in the dark(ness)

    On the cool(ness)   of the lining
Meeting the   last coin

    He held / in lyric flesh   reformulating our time
    Together in a room   he is mine

[I GO FROM ROOM TO ROOM]

I go from room to room taming dust,
gathering a corner looking you up

The rooms gather me into their walls
smoothing out hard-to-the-touch nostalgia
the rooms I see are in a no-place

I remember overhearing a philosophy professor
on the subway instruct his son on *utopia*,
he said it was from the Greek,
a word that is no place
because it is nowhere

I am refound in light —

The walls' plaster hardening
like an artery

I put myself inside a family
I keep telling you that, in sleep,
no one can hurt me

LOVE ON THE X-AXIS

If you are alive, somewhere, alive —,   Alone somewhere I cannot reach on foot

Or mechanical wing   Let's talk like we used to

       I say, Papa

If you fail   To understand my   Impoverished Russian

       I will relearn it in twilight   That you existed —,

       That, one day, will be enough for me

TWILIGHT OF NIGHT

Hamlet speaks to the ghost of his father
for advice to avenge his death

I want you to tell me how to live. It is twilight —, again I am without you —.
I used to hear footsteps, the echoing tremors of a bare foot stepping on a wooden
floor. The house still, as though it died, holding its breath waiting for you to
arrive. I want you to tell me that it matters that I am waiting.
I am the observer of all observers. The book of sonnets you left before you left,
I have committed to memory —. I have started rereading Shakespeare's sonnets,
I am stuck on Sonnet 97. I need you to tell me what they mean.

WE ARE ALL ACTORS ON A STAGE STUTTERING BEFORE THE CURTAIN

I'm no Ophelia, my Lord

falling before your feet for the common good,
if only I could mark my body's vessel as my own
putting thee to shame, fair lord

& at times I am the fool
making myself a spectacle before the public square
always doubtful

of what it means to be a woman in Byzantium

constituted of madness,
a mind visited

upon by a single ghost
in the distance, a mother, like poor sight too close

fatherless, I am in my heart not speaking
any language

CHESTNUT TREES, KYIV

Clear / lonely in their dream
Buds not yet floret heads

Defying sunlight
Bloomed with thoughtless flowers

LOVE ON THE Y-AXIS

Depicting with	Pain
Not pen	A female beauty
The way	A man
Tells	A story
In a frame	A still life
	A bowl of vegetables
What	Historians
	Leave out

ARS POETICA

The Dutch school of painters had it right. The way they carved out light, laying it inside
out on the inhabited body of the canvas. The skin of the canvas becoming tissue
like a body being unfolded before the world, before itself —,

The way it opens to the viewer   what is   to the body's ending.

       Each turn, peeling
                              back the light
       in everyone I meet

DEATH OF VENUS

I had to shield myself
from beauty to survive it.
Waywardly, we made our
way to Rome. Did I mistake
our pause for a holiday in Italy?
I was a girl, I went everywhere
she'd take me. On Saturdays
to the Vatican, Rome's main
post office to collect letters
from my father & mail our
letters to him. After we left,
he moved in with my maternal
grandparents in Kyiv for what
felt to all — palliative / urgent care.
Across the street, the twelfth-century
cathedral kept to itself, shy in gilded
theology. Her father, a decorated
officer in the Red Army.
Her mother cooked like a Michelin-
rated chef. The three of them
eventually ghosts in gold leaf.
After dinner, my grandfather
playing Schubert on the baby
grand. My fiery dangerous
memories. Three objects
of beauty.
       On the train back
to our practically priced apartment
for Soviet immigrants (thirty minutes
to anywhere), my mother read
his letters like Pushkin's lovesick
Tatyana on that fevered night she
wrote Onegin her youthful, foolish
love letter. I looked on & on, on

moving grottos occupied by livestock.
Italianate pastorals. Train travel bores &
pains me. First: the monotony of thuds,
jumps like the needle off track on
a vinyl record, skipping its way back
on track. Second: *The violence of parting.*
My father waving us off on a hill forever.
Third: my entry through the train window
to banality of family suffering.
Doing nothing especially special.
Waiting. Waiting. Waiting.
Inside the Sistine Chapel (in the
the archipelago of theological &
administrative buildings) in
Vatican City. Encountering
Michelangelo's *Last Judgment*
wall fresco, up the steps
inside the vault, on our Saturday
visits. My mother reassuring
me that the suffering of the
damned is a creative project.
In the right corner, Charon
ferrying the dead to the
underworld. Would he take
my father away, I wondered,
denying a dying man's wish
to be with family & friends?
                    Was my mother
hopeless? Did she believe this to be
our only time together in Italy?
I have been back a handful of times.
At twilight, my Margot just two, in the stroller
facing Rome (pickpockets, bats above us
navigating down for prey) drew out.

Behind the lip, Margot, untouched,
safe with me.
                    Was my mother
afraid I would be stolen in plain sight,
in daylight? How would she report me
missing in hysteria of Russian?
She held on to my hand everywhere
we'd go. Like a pearl diver holds her
breath deep underwater. My wish:
to be back with my mother on our
Roman holiday. While she still had
the letters, while she stayed alive.
                    It was on a trip
to Florence —
I was in love with my father.
(I am still in love with him)
His love letters for us. My mother,
in step with me —
I dressed in flared denim, Roman
gladiator sandals, my own copper
hair at a standstill when I saw her
rising out of the Uffizi's marbled
floor. I saw her as Botticelli
(her maker) — intimately, in
Birth of Venus. She invited me in,
tenderly at ten. I could see myself
in her. Alive. Away from adult
problems. Beauty saved me.
A maiden before the mark
of puberty. Small breasts
on the rim of beginning of skin.
The shell, her permanent room —
porcelain & compact

like a woman's
mirrored pressed-powder
case. Her dead hair,
depressed down. Her
voluptuous belly, before
puberty, before marked
as someone's again. Before
the fall. Her copper hair
covers her navel. The dream
the museum visitors could
not make overnight. She would
do away with sleeping.
Let her hair fall heavy like water,
dripping from a rarely used faucet.
The self, unmade overnight,
stubbornly clinging to symmetry
of stanzas. Moving us away
from that overnight train
from eastern to western
Europe. Cutaways of train
platforms stretching out before
the eye, like sunburned skin.
From wheat fields to cities.
The private sleeping car
my mother procured
rocked us to sleep like a cradle
to a hum of parting.
Moving in & out of
memory. I wasn't old
enough to live for myself.
The Uffizi's made-up air,
smothering her visitors —

PAHA (NOUN, RUSSIAN)

WOUND

CHICAGO, SUMMER 1979

We spent a year in Chicago, our final destination, without Father. I'm sure we ate a lot of McDonalds for good & bad reasons. I was learning English — on the fly. *Sanford & Sons* in cultural discordance & dissonance filled my afternoons. The troika of *Three's Company* taught me

that desire can be made. In exile, Father was obscured by his disease. He sold furniture for rubles with almost no value. Mother gave her collection away of the Russian canon to a good friend. Literature was eschewed, sent away like dissidents to the Gulag. I spent much of my time that summer away from mother at the local JCC, swimming

I rode my bike to the lake in the afternoons. My mother couldn't manage dollars, half / broken half / broke. My father, a refusenik, on trial — in debate with death. He was acquitted of a crime he didn't commit. He made it out of a closed country, half / alive, let go to die with us — a year & a half later. My mother was never barren

AT THE BEAUTY SHOP WITH MY MOTHER II

She loved hair. In strands, cutting her off from poetry
She loved more. She knew by heart from grade school.
Recited at evening salons at home when she married my father.
When they argued about the work being beneath his station in
Society, she declaimed that *it's like making poems, or teaching
Russian,* her university studies. *It is what she did for extra money.*
Women came & went on Saturdays & Sundays. Lacking tension,
She performed hair miracles under four 50s-style hair dryers
(The only ones on the market) that lined the long corridor
Of our (single-family, non-communal) Brovary apartment.
Women left in Mireille Mathieu night-black silky / short
Long weaves / wigs / hand-woven / real hair; Hitchcock
bleach-blond buns / smoothed down / sprayed to immovable glossy.
Proclivities-of-the day, rustled in her hands like book pages she re-read nights.
                                        In summertime, a terminal
Wind from the kitchen, terminated inside their hand-made
Cotton dresses, they copied out of Soviet home economics
Journals. Faithful to each cutting. Worn without a slip.
The hardness / stiffness of new cotton, snared the heat
Between puffy thighs. By day *comrades of industry* (space
Engineers, math teachers, classics professors) alongside
Men; by night, my mother's customers metamorphosed
Into soft-skinned, small-waisted, soft-spoken, wives &
Mothers; seeking — Pathos / Love / Palliative
Care. *Sex was the new opium of the people. Free love
The currency.* 60s sensibilities infiltrating the U.S.S.R.
Legal abortion sustaining scarcity /sin.
Free / fecund — suppressing the state's birth rate.
                                        The women shared their troubles
& sold each other black-market, Western contraband. Lancôme
(Smuggled in by Bulgarian businessmen was the preferred skincare
& makeup brand.) Packaged in night-black-glossy-lacquer. Soviet-red

Lipstick, nail polish & night-black mascara, curling up the upper row of eyelashes.
Night-black eye-pencil lined the top lid. Pantyhose in day-nude & night-black.
Each beauty tool achieved its object. For each exoticism blowing
Their meager inadequate salaries, borrowing for the shortfalls
& paying up with joy.
                              My mother gleaning me from
The oval mirror leaning against the wall in the corridor like a person.
Mornings, she applied the routine of beauty to her face; hair teased,
Night-black brows plucked thin to rash-red. Her body overflowing
With the body's misses & regrets. Her hair creations keeping her
From writing poems.
                              My mother was mortally
Afraid. Talking in a downed voice. After supper she read
The Berlitz Russian-to-English travel-size dictionary.
Maybe she told herself, it was just a trip abroad.
She started dieting more & more. Yogurt days, fruit days.
She stopped listening to music. Each night she wrote coded
Letters to my father, narrating America. Hair in a net, her single day
In an inner-city school cafeteria job, plunging food trays down
A depressed conveyor belt. *I am qualified in hair,* she lectured a counselor.
The Chicago unemployment office procured her a job as a shampoo girl
In a neighborhood beauty shop, when the year (on unemployment) ran out.
Divorced / Single / Middle-aged / English-free / Woman
With a child in a foreign country. (One of multitude of humiliations
Enabling us to leave a closed country. *Raskol.* A split on paper.)
                              On weekends, for extra money,
My mother & I cleaned that beauty shop. Adeptly, in its oversized
Windows, it occupied light & hope. Glimmering in mirrors of the
Stylists stations. In rubber gloves, I felt like a housewife in a Comet
Commercial. Wielding my toilet brush in victory over human waste.
Plunging its prop bristles forcefully down & around the porcelain
Bowl of the prop toilet. My mother mopping the floor like an ocean.

My mother obscured. My mother incandescent. My mother restrained.
My mother's paused mind. I keep wondering. Could my mother
Confide in herself. (Beauty to beauty). Reciting poems to herself
When I'm not there to overhear. In sleep's demise. In love's
Companionship. In human unhappiness.

    Washing grief out

                    Of hair

    Before I could hold her

HAND-ME-DOWNS

I don't remember being hung up on his things. After all like our things, they weren't his — they were handed down. Furniture, clothes, all the spoons & forks of the world, having been dumped in our kitchen by a social worker from the Jewish Federation. They were hollow aluminum, lacking weight. They resembled us. & he was weightless. Like he was already outside us. Like he didn't require beautiful cutlery. Charismatic, well-turned out, a handkerchief inside a coat pocket. Why would he need to look turned out — his body assuming zero gravity, as if in preparation. He didn't want the *whatever comes next.* He was fine with the easy, the weighted, the weighed-down world. The white plastic bag the nurse handed us with the clothes he wore that morning.

VOICE OF AMERICA

In the late evenings — at 9 o'clock — right at my bedtime
he would tune in to the distant sounds of *Voice of America*
turning the dial left & right on a shortwave radio, shorting
out the jammers. It was a better kind of propaganda —
one with raspberries sold all year round all over urban & rural
America. In émigré Russe, he heard a Russian that wasn't born
into the proletariat class. The broadcasts existed somewhere
between the pages of a dictionary & a novel. He found
an otherness he craved, a freedom of both spoken & unspoken —
a priori madness of the Soviet kind. He listened for the sounds
of love, the way it was expressed & held. The war played
out in voices outside of history, outside of economic facts.
Capitalism, in its nudity, — *the enslaved idealize enslavement*
he used to say. I don't remember his voice in glowing Russian.
The many recordings he made at Amoco, mother lost or threw away
in a Chicago dumpster in an alley behind our apartment.
A city soldered out of industrial smoke. The ones I interpreted
for him late into evening. The ones that kept him employed.
English would never come easily, it would never come at all.
I saw it all — the slaughter of the slaughtered. My children
know my voice. Would I recognize his —

TIME OF DEATH

Your gown opened as wide as a heart
You gave up a signature beret for a scrub hat
Your breaths got shorter, less coherent

You assumed the role of the patient, the role
I learned by heart. The simplicity of death
is always surprising. Hospitals, overcrowded by it

The linoleum's gloss overwhelms the slight man
holding on to the pole of an IV bag, propelling himself
forward through the liquid stare of the floor

The heart opens & closes. And why is it that you had to
die there, us waiting for some administrator to announce
your time of death like they do in medical TV dramas,

in a declarative English sentence: Grigory Fridman,
the one who couldn't stop loving you, the one
with myriad defects, the one who caused us to bruise

I'm sorry but your father is dead. And there & then
you immortalized the clock

SITTING SHIVA

After the burial, my parents' friends filled our small apartment, at the door washing their hands from a pitcher of water before entering. They brought cakes, cookies — traditionally sweet baked goods to take the sitters out of mourning playing out in real time — as pain played a central role. The Soviet Jew wasn't used to this kind of natural order of things. We were stunned by pain, grown null by its avarice. My sister's & mother's faces were soft & the puffy redness that settled just under their skin seemed like it was always there. They were being rolled, as by a storm, an invisible violence. My sister tore the lapel of the black blazer she gave me to wear, part of a pantsuit. It was new, not a hand-me-down like most of my clothes in those early years as refugees. All I could think was that I couldn't wear my sister's beautiful suit again because it was ruined. I mourned a suit. I would grow into loss much later, after I had kissed a boy for the first time. According to custom, we had to sit on low furniture, but we had stately chairs & sofa, an anonymous donation from a wealthy family. Everywhere I looked, I saw poppies: heads bowed, heads bopping.

RUSSIAN

I decline & conjugate. Nouns, bending to verbs

I AM MY FATHER'S DAUGHTER

I was one with the cold / Moscow imparted, an import
from the old Soviet days / A mixture of mud & snow
on my western-brand boots, / as deep as my animus
after all these human years / loneliness inexpressible
since we left without him / The hotel kept my passport
at the front desk. I wasn't / a flight risk, there, as a tourist.
In love with the man I was there with — his blush, his smell
Co-mingled with mine, from the night together into morning.
Splitting a shy moon into parts / married / not married.
I spent the day in our room / reading, waiting for him.
Through the crack in the window, snow started to accumulate
On the windowsill. / I wanted to get warm, I took the elevator
to the lobby. Ordered black tea / with lemon. It was just the two
of us, a tycoon du-jour, at the bar / in a German-manufactured
suit, an ironed handkerchief inside a breast pocket / He must have
slid off the rose-gold wedding ring / his right ring finger freed.
His wife used to this when / he would come home. His wife
who darns his socks / who washes by hand his underwear
that dries on a short clothesline in / the post-communal
bathroom. His family / descendants of Bolsheviks. As we
locked eyes, he sparkled like / the disco ball affixed to the
celling in the middle of the bar / The mirrors, luminous
celestial bodies / emitting & capturing light with each rotation.
He smacked, rearranged his lips on the vodka / shot as cold
as snow crushed underfoot / Outside, a weather revolution.
His perverse / bristling beauty. A birch forest / between us.
A grotto for *Mother Russia's* beatific love / for her people.
Inside, a closed ideology. I sat there locked / waiting for
something — only *Moscow* could teach me / *Her* in 1917.
Murderous, revolutionary. *Her* imperial seat of government.
(The Duma.) Her, post-revolutionary / where the regime's
politicians (thought up) legislative deviations / He looked

like a technocrat, descending into / middle age without a fight.
Like Anna Karenina's husband / Reliably unimaginative.
With more money than he should / have gotten away with
stealing from the people. Vodka / sweat / swallowing up
his top lip. He looked / like he was drowning —
I could have followed him to his / room after he sent a note
in Russian with the waiter / One vodka shot & beluga
like rare black diamonds / spinning in the crystal dish
a small glass spoon upright / I could have allowed him
to give me pleasure / the Russian kind. Abundant.
Firm as a *kulak* — I could have whispered obscenities
in his ear, a turn-on I'm sure / he couldn't have imagined
from a woman. I could have / taken $1,000 he offered
for the night. The note said — whatever it costs to have me,
he'd pay. I could have made / him crawl on all fours.
For the surveillance crew / listening in on the night.
I could have hurt him / I could have cried in his chest.
A universal language. I learned / & relearned. I could do
it all over again with or / without. Human matters.
In whispered desperation / When I saw the man
I loved. His lapis-lazuli eyes / Our night on his lips.
Our night turned on its head / Our feral love.
How could anyone compete / My living ruin.
Like cells in division / In friction. In one person
diving into another, like a blade / falling on a tree
in a forest. Papa, he could have admired you
stepping into your kind of valediction. He would
be you. How could he compete?

ON BEAUTY, BETRODDEN

Beauty existed. In his beauty. In bitter beauty.
I replace a cobblestone with concrete. Restored to —,

One brick at a time. The path overgrown with a narrowness,
For the hiker. Dissected again without ether or a wayward opiate. As I walk & measure,

Measure myself & walk, against progress —. Against literature
Read & reread, against the ticking of a grandfather clock, against a concrete wall.

Without primal drive, crossing into life. I am unfounded.
My stillness is evolving —.

We watched our moon being pulled apart.
As it parted, extinguished.

ROAR AT WRIGLEY FIELD

In the bleachers at an afternoon game — sun tucked away behind the supporting wall of Wrigley Field — the three of you celebrate baseball in Chicago's biggest hit. I am with him again, somewhere over the rainbow & back to you. I'm reading something important, literature fixed on a smartphone. I am lost in & to large ideas. Love is in the way. He fires arrows relentlessly. My only reliable god. Literature breaks the vertebrae of resolve. I read Pasternak's *Hamlet*. It is an ambitious translation, at times nothing closely resembling the original. Visotsky on YouTube — between plays — echoes the new work of art. The infield is a beautiful stage for America. All around me children capped in baseball caps spin balls *en plein air*. The strikes, the science of the throw. Game theory in play before all of us. Facing things straight on. Hitting things out of the park.

Отчаяние (NOUN, RUSSIAN)

DESPAIR

LENIN

I pen my looming Russian letters, the letters surrendered
to being letters, circling air. The page yielding to October 1917

Letters weighed in grams, as valuable as bread. The architectural
stature of Russian. It was there under glass held in a case. The folds of creases

relaxed on the page. In cursive, under pseudonym of Jacob Richter,
Lenin seeking admission to the Reading Room at the British Museum.

Set out on a pilgrimage one summer, I meant to end
the stroll in the Parthenon Room, bypassing the frieze & minor marble gods

pushing & shoving through history, books thrown in the fire.
Generating little heat for the revolutionary lost in ink,

blotted out by history. The yoke is still a yoke. The hand that writes
out its own destiny. Clause linked to clause. As I wait for you to be mine again

CRIME SCENE

We step into a home, a warm room within another warm room. It has a bed, a sink & room for a table, a step away from his steps. It begins. The performer begins to unleash the flowers of violence, &

*

each morning she wakes up to his absence — it is a morning greeting. The absence anointing to a world missing *existence*. We are each other's mirror, combing out strands of time. The ruins of the soul. I'm waiting. I harvest —, pain one root at a time. Deflowering the roots,

*

I am beginning to think & look at the world like you. To talk like you. To sink in deep sinkholes like you. Purse my lips like you. Wear sorrow around my neck like you. Reflect my face in the opaque lit-by-broken-moon-in-water-in-the-brook like you. It runs deep & wild like you,

I let in deletions as unwelcome guests make visitations. Long-distance travelers from a deleted world into a deleted world. I have too much to lose if I let them stay too long. Mathematically speaking —, *silence + silence* equals *finite silence.* From the father who is — long dead & from a mother who is yet to be dead. A guest is not a roommate,

*

or a body of water pooling into a wave. We stood, my puppy & I — her ears like antennae — & I was being guided to look at a fleeting, flickering moment; the brook lit up by a blunt moon — as it unfolded in the dark darkness, the light cutting the darkness in long cuts,

*

we didn't hear her imaginary footsteps —, we saw her! A lissome apparition of a red fox — she ran in & out of the imagined emptiness, in & out of a neighbor's front yard more quickly than a dog, then turning a corner. Becoming invisible.

IN THE LIGHT OF THE MOON

Not words / I wish for / Eyes meeting – Babi Yar, Yevgeny Yevtushenko 1961
И мне не надо фраз. / Мне надо, / чтоб друг в друга мы смотрели

I
My father brings me to the heart
Of the old Jewish cemetery
Where I'm near the dead.

A pack of boys, in holocaust attire.
Wild with happiness. They looked like
Uncentered rocks. Babi Yar in a summer haze
Light dimming on her surface. Steps away,
Look how a boy is warming up a frozen leaf
Cupping what's left of it in his veinless hand.
Clinging to his mother, he faints
Into the mouth of the ravine.

There, a baby
Feeds on a woman's dead breast
As he suckles on death.
The ghost of father tells me to remember
Them as tones culled out of water. We place stones
As tears that turn into stones.

II

It is winter.
The clotted-clay soil isn't opening
Their bodies aren't open

Lifting the stone page
The moon leads me unwilling
On this third day of her fullness of Passover
Away from Kyiv
Where my grandmother's mother   is felled

They are taking the first-born
& the second & third
As I stand with him reviewing graves

III

        2 adults

My great-grandmother

A   daughter   my great-aunt

3   children

                   2   girls 6 & 4

                   1   boy of 1

They stand before the mouth of the ravine
The dirt hardens
Like the 33,771   on September 29 & 30   1941
They are   being returned

The void opens
As wide as a yawn
A baby's finger is stuck in a closed
Button in search of a blind thread
An old Jew's grandson is bayoneted
The old Jew's voice isn't letting out anything
That is human. A boy is speared,
The old Jew opens his hands up to that void above him —
And says a prayer he says each Sabbath:
Barukh ata adonai eloheinu melekh ha'olam
Blessed are you, our god, the one who commands
The multiverse. *The mourner's kaddish*
Is for the living, the voice says.
It sways east.

Light separates from light,
Yit'gadal v'yit'kadash sh'mei raba
May their name grow in praise,
B'al'ma di v'ra khir'utei
In the garden they fabricate
As they will

They accompany luggage
Packed with socks & shoes

Their father, a small-town rabbi,
Begins to recite the verses from kaddish

WHISPER IT TO ME

here on the edge of everything   I ride in & out of wishful thinking
I've spent my life braiding   ropes in one room & dying in another

without him

in my rooms   he keeps me
unbraiding rope   from rope

here on the edge of everything   I ride in & out of wishful thinking
I've spent my life braiding   ropes in one room & dying in another

without him

in my rooms   he keeps me
unbraiding rope   from rope

AN ACCIDENT OF THE IMAGINATION

It's true I never write, but I would gladly die with you.

— Franz Wright

0

Deep in the nursery's flora section, I saw it. I would have missed its small forest imprint; its small beauty; how it made itself present in plain sight. In miniature splendor, it kept its interior from me.

*

In my retelling, I am losing something.

*

For so long I believed it was

a rare flower my father let me discover

for myself in a forest under mushroom & pine.

*

In Kyiv, so long ago now, he brought the three
of us on International Women's Day, a spring flower,
gathered outside our backyard forest.

*

He a young father gathering unsparingly, bright, in my emptiness.

*

Four years before I was born, he was already sick.
he fell asleep after dinner on the sofa watching TV,

up to him like a sentinel —

*

Often, when
I would sneak

62

with one ear to his heart, almost sounding like mine

It was beating,

*

when I ran up the steps home after playing.

& that's all

Sometimes, I would check for his chest to lift

I cared about.

up

like a lid on a pot.

The same movement Margot's & Finley's chests made when they were babies.

*

All I cared about was for them to keep breathing —

for them to survive

babyhood.

63

I

It's dark in my emptiness, to hold him – my brain grew &
it structurally can't hold him —

*

When I was next to your heart when I was a baby. & you're gone &
I have to live — with that.

*

& that you will never get to love Margot & Finley like I do you —

*

My brain grew out of you & I can't forgive myself because I learned not to forgive you.

Who did you fuck on your trips to Bulgaria? Was it Maria with green eyes & a scar above her lip? Or Masha with an afterglow of a rabbit?

*

Leaving a crater in the living room. Bella busting out in all directions.

The mother of the womb.

*

& on your return bring us Western gifts & deploy kisses like nuclear arsenal on your nuclear family.

*

I hope the pleasure of polyamory eased your (in)constant pain.

The heart, loins, what does it matter?

*

I don't care about your betrayal of my mother that much!

*

You're my dead dad & I know you didn't plan to die.
        I can't get over it. I have three people who I love with a *terrible beauty*.

& of course, Bella is living.
        & I love god for this small kindness.

3

The clerk, whose earring dangled in despair
on her ear placed in the shallow part of my car
trunk three plastic containers

of *lily-of-the-valley,*

the very spring flower that you told me
was hard to cultivate outside a forest. In exile
requiring canopy for shade.

I dug three small holes, with a bronze hand shovel
slipped in each a measuring cupful of ethically-made organic soil
& planted the flowers
in pre-bloom

It took two years for the florets to break
through & hold themselves up to light

& each spring I patrol my garden, I kneel
to smell their unctuous perfume

& I leave them in soil & move on to something else to cut
down & bring inside

Deep in my heart, we are home
I introduce you to my family

MEASURING DISTANCE THROUGH CLOSENESS

I sit and wait —,
sidestepping the abyss
until *this* becomes *that.*

And *that* disappears —.
And if you tell me you love me from this side
and that side as wide as the mouth opens,

I will start burning my books.
And I will make you unsafe with me,

ERASURE, POLICE PRESS RELEASE

02/07/1981

***

[CHILD] SEXUALLY ASSAULTED IN ROGERS PARK: POLICE;

CHICAGO — A serial rapist is invisible to us. Police issued a warning after a ~~woman~~ [child] ~~said she~~ ~~was~~ sexually assaulted in the Rogers Park neighborhood

Police said a ~~31-year-old woman~~ (a child) was walking on the ~~6600 block of North Clark Street~~ ~~around 6:40 p.m.~~ [5600 block of Devon Avenue around 3:20p.m. Wednesday [maybe Thursday] ~~when a man approached her from behind, grabbed her and put his hand over her face~~ [when a man ran behind her into the vestibule of the apartment building and put a knife at her throat]. Police said

██ ; she lost consciousness was awake.

██ ████ , ████ .

Police described the man ████ however, no further description was provided.

Police are reminding the public to be aware of their surroundings and to pay attention to ██ ████ people ██ the area and to report them to officials.

Anyone with any information about the incident should contact the Bureau of Detectives Area North at 312-744-8261.

— END —

70

SEAGULL

she *observes**absorbs* / in a *curved* line / a seagull *curling sea**air* / a *woosh* / *harming* her ear
out of my parents' eyeline   I'm   *building* a sand castle / heavy as a fever

[*creature* / *grant me* / *this small hope*]

I'm free & safe like Chekhov's Nina on her childhood lake in *The Seagull*
I'm going to destroy you for I have nothing better to do

rooted to evil flowers
I used to take my walks in ivory towers
my summers on that greasy lake
what love couldn't take or break
returned a marvelous mistake

what love couldn't take or break
returned a marvelous mistake
I used to take my walks in ivory towers
rooted to evil flowers
my summers on that greasy lake

an old-fashioned death

that *avian*body's
my*body*onthepage

lift & drag
in the *visitors*seagull's sight*grip*

in one swoon
I'm in possession
on his command I don't dare vocalize my voice

in slow motion / the seagull / sounds a long*warning*call to competitors
in a cycle of *higher*pitched / longer*notes* / shortening / descending

it slows at the point of water's blindness
*clutches*clenches me
*feet*dancing for a longtime into liftoff

MEMORY OF A 14-YEAR-OLD GIRL

When I make a fist   the hot mess of it   breaking with gravity

She teaches me   to destroy   the things I love —,

A CONSCIOUSNESS

what do
I call it
at my
neck?
all that
glitters,
in a hand
that stopped
~~a teen~~
like a pause
between
life &
death
a day at school
like any other
after sex
what? what
you have
made.
~~a kill~~

ON THE OTHER SIDE OF BEAUTY

0

I latchkey the lock heavy as an ocean. One turn to the left / Click / the door unfurls, allowing entry to my lurksome visitor. He ricochets *the body of us* into my bedroom — the family dining room —

Bed / Supine / Senses / Defenseless / Heart / Desist / Deceased

1

Behind him my bed, stripped naked to the mattress. My underwear, & bed sheets confiscated by a detective. The room deleted from the cerebral cortex malformed in an adolescent's brain, one unable to see pain through an abstract apparatus —

2

After the hospital, I overhear a private conversation between my father & mother. Echoes of echoes swallowing the texture of time — time withheld from itself. My father lusterless like an old photograph, at the dining table, washing down sorrow & a fistful of heart pills —

3

The room refracts an outline of a family. Dust collects inside its corners. The three people living here, create a culture. Roomful / Uncompanionable. *Meaning moves / Anxiety / Loss / Shame*

From here on in & out, this is my life —

FRONTMATTER

How can I let you in on *this*
It's just that this is unequal pain
The kind that waits for you
The kind that hunts you down
Outside of ideas you hold dear
You say make music
Aren't you Russian enough
You the one whose torso
Is made of diffuse snow
The one who looks
More like a scarecrow
Than a *snegurachka*
My mother sewed all my dolls'
Clothes from leftover fabric
Of my day dresses & costumes
She taught me how to cut
Out with precision right angles
Rounding out stubborn threads
Each breath an act of vengeance
There is always another voice
Behind the part of the brain
That won't let go
Deleted matter

DRUNKEN NIGHT FOR TWO VOICES

— after Berlioz's *Nuit d'ivresse et d'extase infinie, Les Troyens*

[Prologue]

Sunk in darkness, out of which, the voice that's voiceless grasping to become a cord

The male voice pleads for the night to keep its darkness full

Her wrist on his throat feeling for the tremble of the vocal cords

in French, chords cording

The voices are too female & too male

trapped inside the night —.

[Act I]

We are not in my delirium

on your knees on the hardest surface

of our floor —. You ask me for something important to you —,

(You is abstract & specific, it's a beloved, a lover, a father, a warrior)

*

*

you are swelling up with our violence

You grow louder —, shifting me in gravity

I keep vigil for my dead; my dead breathe our air. The air isn't ours to push. The dark covers you so

suddenly. You vanish suddenly. It wasn't long, just for

a moment in time,

which for us is an eternity.

If the universe were a plant —, it would make itself stop growing & bearing fruit

You must feel ashamed of this small transgression —,

(*Against You*)

Why won't you speak to me —

Silence has no path, you should be making one toward me, as dark as the light is between two bodies

rounded out by longing

(Against Aeneas)

Somewhere, the Middle

[Act II]

A man's suffering is more beautiful than a woman's

I watch yours like a Tarkovsky move on film — a black or a white horse falling down before a

prophesy —, buckling & bowing at someone's invisible feet

It feels like something is letting my blood, siphoning it off in gulps

Scene after scene

at last seeing what is invisible here in vivid darkness

*

The shield his mother bore

It's still alive —,

And the distance is mine

father's dead shadow is alive

In the darkness that obliterates the memory of his abridged life

I am a master of violence

(*Against my male figures*)

*

Aeneas & Dido are heartbreaking

(*How they break in me*)

Aeneus follows his destiny to found Rome

(*Let's watch her body's ambers die*)

Dido drives Aeneas' sword into her diaphragm as she walks into the fire

The sword casts a light & shadow

Aeneus follows her into the fire until he recoils from its elements

(The gods have spoken)

*

Dido loves

& burns half-alive in the fire

*

Aeneus abandons Dido, Queen of Carthage

He flees from her love to found Rome

(the gods have ordained it to be)

[Épilogue]

I can hear silence in its voiceless cord, a nocturne in G flat major

I didn't learn to read music

The language of gaps & pauses

Timing —, the shame is mine alone

Time isn't going to heal all wounds —,

*

A stray child too is there rising out of fertility

(Venus, Aeneas's mother, a god, commissions a shield for her son)

(The last ekphrastic scene, Aeneus's walk down to the underworld)

Walking down overgrown grass rising to heaven —, or maybe to its opposite.

I am never sure. I'm not sure of anything. We're lost inside our own rules. Snow & ice yield to

the overheated chords. The child runs toward a figure that looks like a young mother,

with luster in her loins —.

*

The daggers being caught inside her are just daggers, which when at last extracted
will become daggers –

Everywhere it is as violent as when the world began in one outburst

The night unable to move the insects in flower beds to sleep
Its dangling flowers stilling in despair's lows

*

The reasons for ensuring the night unfolds.
In such a night —, I am outside myself
Taking my final leave, leaving for good all the good that I've known —, & I am grown

Who am I in you. My one side is mine, another is yours. Is it really music. No,
I refuse to make
it with you.
(*My music is mine. My discordant chords.*)

What dawns on me —,

INSTRUCTION MANUAL FOR A RAPE

"Ask, now that *body* shines no longer, by what light you learn"
—"b o d y," *A Scattering of Salts*, James Merrill

*

Briefly, she's the fittest vertebrate
Intimate with an alien
Crossing normal, human unhappiness

*

How she let him break her open
[Disprove the earth isn't flat, over & over]
The heavens have no weather

*

Woody thorns sprouting from living, connective tissue
[Render her useless to herself]
An apple orchard overgrown with unique tenderness

*

A hush looping through a wired telephone —
[Tutor her on self-loathing]
The call to the other side of the girl's steadfast mourning

*

[Propel her through the field of relativity]
Banged up, bent space of *dark matter*
Undetected /Unsafe / Holes

       *

[On the way out, inform her: "If you call
The police & tell them about what happened,
I will kill you & your parents. I am watching!"]

       *

[Rely on Einstein's equations. Solve for the Unknown.]
Big Bang's faraway *distortions of light*
As non-luminous as the girl's Pale/Pale skin —

HOME

The Return

How do you record illness that is imposed, that is
extra-existential, that is —
that one day you wake up a historically significant
artifact: the brain before a crime.

0

Concealing longing of one in exile, in longing I weep for him
He was an immigrant for a short time, once an immigrant always
An immigrant with seams like scars unraveling in the open
A mother tongue became a learned stranger.

In Brovary, a feudal Ukrainian city, he read Solzhenitsyn
In samizdat. Dog-eared, thin pages chronicling the empiricism
Of suffering in concentration camps of the Gulag Archipelago
Tundra forests hiding silence,

1

The linear plainness of the Midwest.
Its vast sprawling endless flatness,
Stretching farther than my eye sees.
Our arrival at O'Hare. We were met

By father's best friend & his wife. We
Lived with them in fury. They were more
Acclimated to the flat English vowels they
Were learning in ESL classes for immigrants.

2

It was May, the sun was looking down
On us, Soviet immigrants
Whose belongings were divided into 16 carry-ons,
Mother's brainchild

We transported emptiness & wounds brought
From a country of invented realism, an experiment
In failure possessing the family
Like dispossessed vagabonds

3

I remember the surface stretching for miles,
Nothing beneath it but a 2-dimensional surface
The depth & sense we left behind with him
In our apartment alongside a wheat field

A cornfield outstretched in *The Chicago Tribune*
On the front page Carter's toothy smile espousing
The *Wheat for Jews* program. Home was an art
Project we left behind with him

4

What was their last night together like?
Two bodies, in happiness & sorrow for the last time.
The distance, the night's blanket.
Alternately sleeping & sleepless. The maker of dreams,

Making visits. Taking & giving. Eyes closed off.
Lake Michigan became our Dnieper, though deeper, darker
& more distant. Its banks drawing in the universe of two.
It spat us out, it spat. Forgetting the taiga, tundra

5

& the steppe's long goodbye. Home is the cave
Cast in long shadows of palms on its walls. In the irrigated
Desert, I collect my wounds. My *oskolki*, pieces of an
Archipelago — making order, out of order. Making water

Out of water. Making ocean water out of
Ocean water. Home is the life-long dig unfolding
In daylight. I am digging, where you are the cover, a body
Covering up a home

Punishment

6

I dig up a garden
From poor, rocky soil — a shallow bed for home
God, is, existence: a wound
That has harmed love's heart

Don't say *mourning*. It's too psychoanalytic.
I'm not mourning, I'm suffering
& you are condemned to eyewitness, to breathe,
To put in your arms the one you love —

7

Will always love —. Watch him die. Shapeless in death
& there's nothing you can do. My dull exile. My home
Is knowing I will open the door to our apartment & see him
The endless pages of the EKGs, the readings of his heart,

The endless readings — the valleys & those high stabs
The peaks of the heart, striking you down like the first nail
In a coffin. The depth of depth. The readings of his heart —
Were my way in —, to him. Why do you have to go, Father?

8

I'm alive but you're not —
Each morning is the same: the sun is too bright,
The eyes are struck down by blindness. Some sun rays die. One.
Two. Three. Count with me. Won't you? Something you said

Interferes. Trees with their treeness reveal tremors. Absence
Again. Distance again. Nothingness mirroring itself. I repeat
With the precision of knowledge that something is better than
Nothing. As you betray me again. As I betray you again

9

We're even,
Trees are as blind as us,
Our women grow silent in silence
I'm going to destroy him —

Because I have nothing better to do
Razkol, a split of psyche from psyche
You come to faith with all
The will against it that your heart accumulated

10

Covered by tired hands. My hands that work with letters
Smithing them to unfamiliar sounds. Out of step with money,
A church sounding bells on Friday afternoons
The illness the body endures & will endure

As the past & future meet. Illness with its familiarity
Invades & occupies
This body laments the illness the body endures
I sew along the seam of the universe

The Cave

11

I am a descendant of cave dwellers. The cave that confines
The soul to its body. The borders of trees
Inside it. The borders,
Resemblances of trees outside it

The cave is like skin over
The eyes: luminous & half-transparent
I will always love my cave
& that nothing resembles it

12

Those who remember the cave. Those who are a ruin,
Are ruins of the cave. The cave is a ruin. Distance is the currency
Of the cave. The dwellers of the cave measure the world inside it.
They communicate with a light they cast on the walls of the cave

The light is estrangement. The light is made out of light
This is a dialogue between me & my dead father. Remember me
Like this. The fire consumes the shadows. I burn a
Requiem candle which has no shadow. It burns my reality

13

Here, water boils on the edge of the edge
The borders on all sides are hot. I serve tea to

Myself — such a dark fragrance-like fragrance
Itself. I'm sipping it at the sipping point,

At the heat point
I'm not soliciting truth in the slim face of the cave,
A dim light reflected in his eyes
My eyes, her eyes

14

The self-corrections & self-regulation
& if the world takes its last breath,
I will have to turn away, turn my face to look away
My pajamas collection, each in white is growing

In more sleep. The way of my survival
I am planning my survival. Each day the plan breaks
Down. Each day survival breaks down. But I keep adding
To my collection of white

15

In what is the opposite of light, I am contained,
Held. Exiled. Back into the cave
Why drag yourself out of the shadows cast in gold,
Reflecting deep gold, warming up to darkness
Safely unmoved & unmoving. The warm glow
Of darkness, is, all there is. The sun is dead
The madman proclaims. His new madness worn
Out like madness

16

You must know changing the soul's
Desires is wrong. Change
The sun's. Okay.
Darken its bright glow to meet

The soul's. Yours. The ill are consumed
With illness there. They have nothing to turn away
From. The trees will be trees. Fire will burn with fire.
And why leave the cave now that you are here with me.

17

Chained, she walks to her wall & draws an object
That looks like the sun: It's round, with imitative rays
Pushed into the cracks of the cave, burnished
To a fiery, sunny yellow.

then hot tears fell,
All cries of mourning
he forbade them, sick at heart therefore
In silence

LETTER

My dearest Papachka,

You would know me if you held on to memory without the hippocampus.
I hope the contents of your memories were transferred after your short
stay with us, your family. I have red hair & your eyebrows framing my
almond-shaped eyes, like yours — calculating danger. Are you living another
spontaneous life? I am —, in the imagination.

Your lovers are dead. My mother has found happiness with a pianist.

Who are you with? Are you allowed to network outside the
immediate circle? You had differences with you mother. She kept my mother
in the snow. You love Uncle Mitya endlessly. Are you with him? And your
father, the listener?

I am in touch with your sister. She uses a desktop computer. She
lives alone in Coney Island, the Atlantic steps away. She wants to give me
the other half of your letters —, the ones you mailed from Rome. Each
envelope stamped with Michelangelo. Your instructions on mailing yourself
parcels from Kyiv to Rome were helpful to her. I didn't know you to be so
practical. You used to spend too much money on whatever you could get your
hands on. Did you visit the museum at the Vatican after you picked up your
own parcels at the post office? I have seen the Sistine Chapel twice. To the
amusement of angels.

How do you manage your moods? Do you meditate?

I write when the moon is neediest. I wrote a poetry collection
collecting you, but I can't publish it. The earth is dying. I miss foraging for
mushrooms in our Russian forest.

The River Styx is in a climate crisis. It's frozen in parts that take one's
breath away. How will I be conducted to you?

At parting, I am consoled by writing. Please let me know if you have trouble reading this letter. It is composed on a laptop, my penmanship is difficult to make out. I cannot make sense of it, it represents the void. Do you go to Einstein's lectures? He must have figured it all out, but god doesn't care.

You don't write! I will wait —.

Your Hayis,

P.S. Write me on Mondays, it's my lightest day.

MOTHER

On sick days before I would wake up to a sickly dawn, I would stay in bed, watching the school bus flicker yellow. When no one would emerge from our apartment building, it would contract its single door, moving on to pick up adolescents from families with a father & a mother. How she would make it worth my while, spooling air into knots. I would wait for her to bring me, on a white porcelain tray, my morning cereal, black tea with 4 teaspoons of sugar & grocery-bought milk chocolate. When she would shut the door behind her, mother's motherness would penetrate the seams of my bed sheets. She was like a German governess, laundering sheets, preparing my food — erasing the day. It was all I knew. I remembered sounds of sprawling legs in the sky. I walked into the night without knowledge. I am left with her —

FATHER

The photograph held for too long in an acid-free frame fell
from the dresser, breaking the glass as if it were hit by a bolt
of lightning. We're in Kyiv, surrendered to gravity —

You held my hand intensely on that ungrotesque day in May,
like only a father can. You were a member of a failed ideology.
And brought me along to the parade,

to counterweigh your burden. You were showing me off
in my May Day best. Starched bows in my hair & knee-high socks.
The sun pausing & starting over. Years later uncovering the family

car from snow. You were returned to us. February grimaced.
Out poured white crystals. Stiff like frozen dirt. The car was parked
on a tree-lined street called Greenleaf. The leaves

absent. Old snow overwhelmed the street. The air preyed on our
lips with a ferocity of a hawk. The air struck the lung in a gesture
of fire. The ubiquitous wheat fields were just beginning to rise

toward the sun. Spring encroached on winter.
Your body unraveled on the concrete like hair out of a stiff
ribbon. The cold obstructed my breathing. On this grotesque

winter day. You surrendered being my father. And I the claim
of belonging to you. Nothing between our palms but air —
I held your hand in mine, like only a daughter can

AFTERWORD

On the anxiety of arriving at *Father Elegies*, the title for the book, honoring my late father, and coming out with my secret (shame).

The book is a kind of thought experiment; in my bringing my father to life, if only in these pages. I am acting against laws of the universe; what Einstein calls*, gedankenexperiment,* an experiment carried out in thought only; against a strict focus on *that which can be measured*. Little is being measured in the book's imaginings. It is an unsatisfactory act of imagination & will — a sonata, a serenade, a series of arias, re-imaginings, re-experiences & re-experiencing, re-loving, re-living, *if onlys*; in restricted form, in free form, the attack on form, the dissolution & disillusionment of form; out of time, — and to no end, with only, *Wound, Misfortune, Despair,* its three movements.

Deciding on a title, before turning in my final draft, proved to be impossible. The relationship between father, language, and identity created a conundrum. I couldn't hold, in a title, the totality of my late father. I had more than a page of possibilities, none expressing in one title my pathos. Possible Titles: *The Impossibility of the Father, Be Mine* (line from poem "Lenin"), *Valediction Forbidding Mourning* (John Donne), *Your Kind of Valediction* (line from poem "I am My Father's Daughter"), *An Accident of the Imagination* (name of poem)*, Your Face Out at Sea* (line from poem "Water" I took out of the book), *The Weighted, Weighed Down World* (from poem "Hand-Me-Downs," second title), *Nowhere with Him* (original title).

A breakthrough one evening at Met Opera in New York. As I watched Verdi's *Un Ballo in Maschera,* in the fall of 2023 with Lily Kaylor Honoré, it became painfully clear that I could never get (him) right. How could I? I knew him for fourteen years, with a child's brain, an emotional coexistence that couldn't be easily plotted or represented in a timeline.

I am my Father's Daughter, emerged in office hours with Terrance Hayes at the graduate creative writing program at NYU in December 2023, as he *marked up* in red, blue & green (the artist & poet always interactive) the poem in the last draft; it was called, *On the Other Side of Beauty,* which he didn't see as a fitting title. I muttered & mumbled, while he drew out the poem's shortfalls; my resistance to hearing what the poem wanted to be. This poem was a late but a balancing addition.

I have long admired Rilke's *Duino Elegies,* which took him more than a decade to complete. It took me a lifetime to write this book, I'm calling, *Father Elegies,* but just sixteen months to complete. An elegy is a poem of both lament & love; I am lovesick & despairing for my father.

Coming out with shame (my secret). It was a hard decision, a debate with myself. I debated whether adding the six poems to *Despair,* the last movement, would distract readers from my father, the subject and object, of the book. Is this the place and time for this I kept asking myself? Since the book is about my father. But the book is also about me in context of the story of my father. About the aftermath on our family, my mother. We didn't get the chance *to cope with it as a family* because he died suddenly soon after. These are the six poems that *create an opening in the void,* a way of introduction, a beginning, of talking about the story of my sexual assault at home by a serial rapist in our neighborhood. "Crime Scene," (p. 54), "Erasure, Police Press Release" (p. 69), "Seagull" (p. 71), "A Consciousness" (p. 73), "On the Other Side of Beauty" (p. 74), "Instruction Manual for a Rape" (p. 84).

The chief reason for my reluctance to include the six poems: I have been protecting my children from the knowledge of my personal history, for a time that they (and I) would be more ready to hear it. Now that they're older, one child is fragile. One child is less so. I worry. I hope I am making the right decision.

Before the book's publication, I will tell them. I waited long enough. They know something else is wrong.

People who suffer sexual assault feel shame. I'm not saying that it's right or wrong. I just do. I am loath to generalize, or speak for others. *It is how I feel.* I have talked and talked and talked about it with my therapist for the last five years. I didn't talk about it for decades to anyone, just to the few closest to me. I wanted to forget it. I wanted it to unhappen. If I did, maybe, it would bring my father back to life. If I did, maybe, he wouldn't have died. It broke his heart. I believe he was ashamed of me, instantly. I believe he was ashamed of himself for not protecting me. I couldn't accept any of it.

The full story will be explored in a memoir-in-poems, I am writing that I hope to publish one day. I am certain in my belief that without the six poems about the secret, the missing piece of the puzzle for me and readers alike, *Father Elegies* would be incomplete.

I resist the solely psychosexual (Freudian) reading of the book, with its trappings & resolutions; the libido (instinct) focus on human drives. The oedipal stage when the child identifies with her mother and the little girl falls in love with her father; the little girl has to come to the realization that he's in love with her mother. And that's the rub.

It's tempting to put on a pedestal a dead person, least of all, one's father. I had to manifest a human being — with all his human qualities. I had to manifest my own along his. I hope I have succeed, if only, in some small way.

Thank you for coming on my journey with me.

Stella Hayes
January 9, 2024

NOTES

My Russian-to-English translation of this abridged version of *Serdze (Heart)*, p. 11, a Russian song popularized by actor & singer Leonid Utyosov, which first appeared in the 1934 Soviet musical film, *Jolly Fellows*.

"Shooting arrows at the heart shot instinctively" (p. 15). *Instinctively* is a style of aiming in archery; a heart shot is aimed at the heart of an animal/mammal target. (Source: phillyarchery.com).

"Razluka" (p. 16) means separation in Russian.

"Dark Night, (Тёмная Ночь), Her Song" (p. 17) is my translation of a WWII Russian song made popular by Soviet actor & singer Mark Bernes.

Raketa (Space Rocket — p. 22) is a Soviet Watch Factory established in 1961 in honor of the first manned flight in space by Yuri Gagarin.

I am the observer of all observers (p. 26). This line, slightly modified, is from *Hamlet*; Ophelia's soliloquy in Act 3, Scene 1.

A modification to the title "We Are All Actors on a Stage," (p.27) quoting Shakespeare, my mother, would often say.

"Chestnut Trees, Kyiv" (p. 28): Kyiv is the capital of Ukraine. My family & I lived an hour outside of Kyiv. I spent many weekends with my maternal grandparents in Podol, a historically Jewish neighborhood in Kyiv.

In "Chicago, Summer 1979," *refusenik* (p. 37) refers to a Soviet political dissident or anyone who is refused to leave the U.S.S.R.

In "At the Beauty Shop with My Mother II" (p.38) *Raskol* means "a split,

a crack, a break." Notably used by Dostoyevsky in the novel *Crime &*
Punishment to name Raskolnikov, his protagonist. Note the prefix Raskol.

"Voice of America" (p. 42). The influence for the line: *the enslaved, idealize*
enslavement is from Boris Pasternak's *Doctor Zhivago*.

"Sitting Shiva" (p. 44) — according to Jewish custom, the bereaved find
loving comfort in gathering at home for seven days of structured mourning,
where family & friends drop in to comfort the mourners.

"I am My Father's Daughter" (p. 46) — in several Eastern and Northern
European countries, e.g., Ukraine, Russia, Poland, Bulgaria, and Denmark, it
is customary to wear a wedding band on the right hand.

"Roar at Wrigley Field" (p. 49): Vladimir Visotsky was a Soviet celebrity:
poet, songwriter Shakespearean & Brechtian actor with a cult following who
performed with the iconic Taganka theater in Moscow. His performance of
Hamlet in the 1970s is widely admired. He is called the Bob Dylan of Russia.

"In the Light of the Moon" (p. 56): According to religious Jewish custom,
Kaddish is a prayer for the dead recited on Yom Kippur, an annual day of
atonement, that is spoken in praise of God. The Yevtushenko epigraph is my
translation from Russian.

"Erasure, Police Press Release," (p. 69): I found a report I had to adapt. In
my research: using the FIA (Freedom of Information Act) with the Chicago
Police, I found nothing about the case or my story. The fourteen girls (me
among them) who were sexually assaulted at their homes (I think so but I'm
not sure) by a serial rapist in our neighborhood. The detectives on the case,
either retired or died. The records not digitized, discarded. It was too long ago,
too much time had passed.

In the poem "Seagull," (p. 71) Trigorin on Nina in *The Seagull*, *I'm going to*
destroy her for I have nothing better to do. I replaced "her" with "you."

Italicized lines in "A Consciousness," (p. 74) are from: *After sex — /…what? /*
What you have made. — Frank Bidart, "The Third Hour of the Night," *Star Dust*

"Frontmatter" (p. 77): miscellaneous pages such as the title & preface that precede the text of a book. *Snegurachka,* Russian for snow princess.

"Drunken Night for Two Voices" (p. 78). In writing the poem, I listened to two recordings of the duet between Aeneas & Dido in Nuit d'ivresse et d'extase infinie! (Night of Rapture and Infinite Ecstasy) at the end of Act 4 in Les Troyens (The Trojans) an aria in G flat major. The two recordings are Strasbourg Philharmonic Orchestra, John Nelson conductor & Metropolitan Opera Orchestra & Chorus, 50 Years at Lincoln Center, a live performance recorded May 7, 2017, by conductors, Marco Armilaito, James Levine, Yannick Nézet-Séguin.

"Instruction Manual for a Rape," (p. 85): "As non-luminous as the girl's pale / pale skin —;" in astronomy, non-luminous objects /celestial bodies don't emit light. Luminosity is the amount of light an object emits in a unit of time.

"Home:" (p. 87): Dnieper is a deep river that runs through Kyiv. It is the 4th longest European river after Volga, Danube & Ural. The passage *Don't say mourning. It's too psychoanalytic. I'm not mourning, I'm suffering* is from Roland Barthes's *Mourning Diary.* The line, *I'm going to destroy him —* is adapted from Chekhov's *The Seagull.* The last stanza of the poem is from *the Iliad. Home is the cave: The reference to the cave is from Plato's Cave as my own cell, home.*

Wheat for Jews Program (p. 88) was a policy — exchanging Soviet Jews for wheat — established, with the support of American Jews, by the Carter administration.

In "Home" (p. 85) the last stanza, *then hot tears fell, / All cries of mourning / he forbade them, / sick at heart therefore / In silence,* is from *The Iliad.*

In "Letter" (p. 94) *Hayis* is joy in Yiddish, one of my father's two endearments for me.

In some poems, removing punctuation at the end of lines is intentional, indicating a continuation of experience across time on the Y & X axes. There is no uniformity in the use of punctuation. Grief creates a different logic and disengages logic; it is permeable, constant, and ever-changing.

ACKNOWLEDGMENTS

I am grateful to the editors of the following publications in which these poems or versions of these poems first appeared:

"Tempera" — The Poetry Project's *The Recluse*

"On Beauty, Betrodden" — *The Hunger*

"The Roar at Wrigley Field" — *Small Orange,* nominated for *Best of the Net 2020*

"Razluka," "Time of Death," "Lenin" and "Voice of America" — Stanford's *Mantis* annual issue 19 (December 2020)

"The Twilight of the Night" — *Poet Lore,* fall 2022

"In Loss's Motion," "Hand-Me-Downs" and "Root Cellar" — *South Florida Poetry Journal*

"Home" — International Human Rights Art Festival (IHRF), *Voices of Ukraine: Impressions Around a War,* April 2022

"Nowhere with Him" (retitled to "[I go from room to room]") and "Chicago, 1979" — *Through Lines Magazine,* inaugural issue (December 2022)

"Letter" — *The Indianapolis Review* (summer 2024)

"Death of Venus" — *Image* (September 2024)

"If Only / If Only," and "At the Beauty Shop with My Mother II" — *Tupelo Quarterly* Issue 33 (September 2024)

Father Elegies, previously titled *The Weighted, Weighed Down World,* was a finalist for the *Possession Sound Poetry Series* at *Poetry Northwest 2022.* The series publishes two select books per year, chosen by the editors during an open reading period. It showcases books that align with the press's mission of supporting musical, language-driven work by established poets.

Nathalie Handal, the book wouldn't exist were it not for you — you are a Rilkean angel. Much love to you!

Dearest David St. John, love always!

Carlie Hoffman, I am deeply grateful for your endless love for me (through thick & thin), for believing in this book too, yet again, and for featuring my work in *Small Orange*.

Terrance Hayes, so much gratitude for your love and commitment to your students; for our long debates on what makes a poem (*it has to have figurative language!*), and how to stay the course.

Poet Elena Karina Byrne for being my gentle What Books Press editor!

Matt Rohrer, for your immeasurable kindness. Love to Sharon Olds for my very first class at the NYU Creative Writing Program; love to Ocean Vuong for my very last, your very first workshop at the NYU Creative Writing Program — I felt & learned so much!

Monica Youn for sharing your brilliance, teaching me to think critically about craft, leaving no stone unturned.

Deborah Landau, for your dedication to the NYU Creative Writing Program, and support.

Zachary Sussman, thank you for all your patient guidance.

Alex Dimitrov, you are celestial — love you!

David Lipsky for teaching tirelessly, the sentence; for living the mantra: *write until you have a first draft*, and Nabokov.

Darin Strauss for office hours, and David Lipsky.

DeSales Harrison for your insights, notes on the book, and generosity of spirit. Erica Wright, thank you for your keen analysis of the book in manuscript, *The Weighted, Weighed Down World,* the working title; and for believing in me!

So much gratitude: Kristina Marie Darling, for all your support & guidance!

Dearest Valentin (1976-2022), our sweet boy, I love you, with all my heart!

Ralph Angel (1951-2020) — that you're at peace.

Rimma "Rimmachka" Kranet (1966-2023), my dearest friend. What I wouldn't do to bring you back to life.

Deep gratitude & love: Marcia Xintaris, Rob Lynn, Lily Honoré, Vika Neznansky, Irina Rubin, Tanya Mallean, Bill Sky, Jason Handler, Nalya Krasnyansky, Gary Light, Sophie Ewh, Quincy Steele, Julia Goldin, Neha Mulay, Amanda Dettmann, Angela Zhao, Kathryn Atwood, Jerome Murphy, Sebastian Doherty, and Maddie Claire Mori.

For unintentionally leaving anyone out, thank you! Many thanks to my fellow poets & writers at NYU MFA Program. And to the staff of *Washington Square Review.*

Joanna Yas for bringing magical, inspiring authors to readings at NYU's Creative Writing Program; for mentoring us & giving us the tools for publishing our work; for your patience, beauty & love.

Gail Wronsky, my publisher at *What Press Books* for publishing *Father Elegies,* my second poetry collection. Thank you to the collective, including Karen Kevorkian, Chuck Rosenthal, Elena Karina Byrne, Gronk, and everyone I have not named. And to the magnificent ash good.

And always for Bella, my mother, Alla, Kushka, Alessa, Dahlia, Dade, Margot & Finley — inexpressible gratitude for your love & love.

STELLA HAYES is the author of two poetry collections, *Father Elegies* (What Books Press, 2024) and *One Strange Country* (What Books Press, 2020). She grew up in Brovary, a suburb outside of Kyiv, Ukraine, Chicago, and Los Angeles. Hayes earned an M.F.A. in poetry from NYU, where she taught in the undergraduate creative writing program and served as poetry editor and assistant fiction editor of *Washington Square Review*. Her work has appeared in *Image*, The Poetry Project, *Four Way Review*, and Stanford University Press, among others. Hayes is a contributing editor at *Tupelo Quarterly*. She lives with her husband and two children in Larchmont, New York.

WHAT BOOKS PRESS

AN IMPRINT OF

THE GLASS TABLE

COLLECTIVE

LOS ANGELES

All WHAT BOOKS feature cover art by Los Angeles painter, printmaker, muralist, and theater and performance artist GRONK. A founding member of ASCO, Gronk collaborates with the LA and Santa Fe Operas and the Kronos Quartet. His work is found in the Corcoran, Smithsonian, LACMA, and Riverside Art Museum's Cheech Marin collection.

As a small, independent press, we urge our readers to support independent booksellers. This is easily done on our website by purchasing our books from Bookshop.org.

WHATBOOKSPRESS.COM

2024

The Manuscripts
KEVIN ALLARDICE
NOVEL

Father Elegies
STELLA HAYES
POEMS

Slow Return
PAUL LIEBER
POEMS

Dreamer Paradise
DAVID QUIROZ
POEMS

How to Capture Carbon
CAMERON WALKER
STORIES

2023

God in Her Ruffled Dress
LISA B (LISA BERNSTEIN)
POEMS

Figures of Wood
MARÍA PÉREZ-TALAVERA
TRANSLATED BY PAUL FILEV
NOVEL

A Plea for Secular Gods: Elegies
BRYAN D. PRICE
POEMS

Nightfall Marginalia
SARAH MACLAY
POEMS

Romance World
TAMAR PERLA CANTWELL
STORIES

2022

No One Dies in Palmyra Ohio
HENRY ELIZABETH CHRISTOPHER
NOVEL

Us Clumsy Gods
ASH GOOD
POEMS

Skeletal Lights From Afar
FORREST ROTH
FLASH FICTION/PROSE POEMS

That Blue Trickster Time
AMY UYEMATSU
POEMS

2021

Pyre
MAUREEN ALSOP
POEMS

What Falls Away Is Always
KATHARINE HAAKE &
GAIL WRONSKY, EDITORS
ESSAYS

*The Eight Mile
Suspended Carnival*
REBECCA KUDER
NOVEL

Game
M.L. WILLIAMS
POEMS

2020

No, Don't
ELENA KARINA BYRNE
POEMS

One Strange Country
STELLA HAYES
POEMS

*Remembering Dismembrance:
A Critical Compendium*
DANIEL TAKESHI KRAUSE
NOVEL

Keeping Tahoe Blue
ANDREW TONKAVICH
STORIES

WHAT
BOOKS
PRESS

LOS ANGELES

Printed in the USA
CPSIA information can be obtained
at www.ICGtesting.com
LVHW050313201124
797134LV00005B/697

9 7 9 8 9 9 0 0 1 4 9 3 0